Library Services for Schools

ERVICES

the last date above. It

D1345266

The Life of
Isambard
Kingdom Brunel

Leonie Bennett

Heinemann
LIBRARY

www.heinemann.co.uk/library

Visit our website to find out more information about **Heinemann Library** books.

To order:

 Phone 44 (0) 1865 888066

 Send a fax to 44 (0) 1865 314091

Visit the Heinemann Bookshop at www.heinemann.co.uk/library to browse our catalogue and order online.

First published in Great Britain by Heinemann Library, Halley Court, Jordan Hill, Oxford OX2 8EJ, part of Harcourt Education.
Heinemann is a registered trademark of Harcourt Education Ltd.

Editorial: Lucy Thunder and Harriet Milles
Design: Richard Parker and
     Tinstar Design Ltd (www.tinstar.co.uk)
Illustrations: Jeff Edwards and Sam Thompson
     (Eikon Illustration)
Picture Research: Melissa Allison and
     Fiona Orbell
Production: Camilla Smith

Originated by Repro Multi-Warna
Printed and bound in China by
     South China Printing Company
The paper used to print this book comes from sustainable resources.

ISBN 0 431 18110 1
09 08 07 06 05
10 9 8 7 6 5 4 3 2 1

British Library Cataloguing in Publication Data
Leonie Bennett
Isambard Kingdom Brunel. – (The Life of)
624'.092
A full catalogue record for this book is available from the British Library.

Acknowledgements
The Publishers would like to thank the following for permission to reproduce photographs:
p. 4 Robert Hallmann/Collections; pp. 5, 13 The Illustrated London News; p. 6 By courtesy of The News, Portsmouth; pp. 7, 26 Bristol City Museum & Art Gallery/Bridgeman Art Library; pp. 8, 9, 10, 18, 20, 22 Mary Evans Picture Library; p. 11 Roger Antrobus/Corbis; p. 14 Fotomas Index; p. 15 David Davis/Collections; p. 16 Scala Art Archives; p. 19 Art Archive; p. 21 University of Bristol; p. 23 Hulton-Deutch Collection/Corbis; p. 24 Milepost 921/2; p. 25 Sally Trussler/Brunel University; p. 27 Bill Meadows/Mary Evans Picture Library

Cover photograph of I.K. Brunel, reproduced with permission of Bridgeman Art Library.
Page icons: Hemera PhotoObjects.

Every effort has been made to contact copyright holders of any material reproduced in this book. Any omissions will be rectified in subsequent printings if notice is given to the Publishers.

Contents

Words shown in the text in bold, **like this**, are explained in the Glossary.

Who was Isambard Kingdom Brunel?

Isambard Kingdom Brunel was one of the greatest **engineers** of all time. He was famous for building railway lines, bridges, and ships.

Isambard was very short. He wore big hats to make himself look taller!

Isambard lived in Britain about 150 years ago. Trains and ships were getting bigger and faster. Isambard was one of the people who made this happen.

In the mid 1800s, People could travel faster on trains than ever before.

A born engineer

Isambard was born in Portsmouth on 9 April 1806. He had two older sisters. His father was a French **engineer** called Marc Isambard Brunel.

This **memorial** is in the street where Isambard was born.

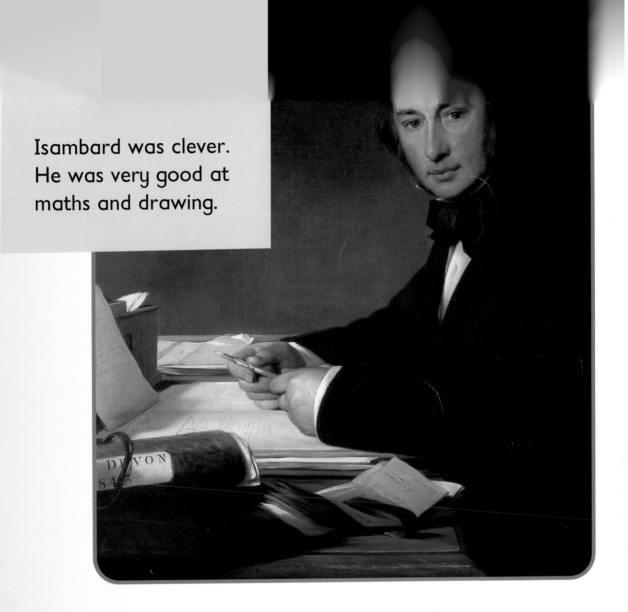

Isambard was clever. He was very good at maths and drawing.

Isambard's father wanted him to be an engineer. He pushed Isambard to work hard. He sent him to a famous school in Paris when he was 11 years old.

Starting work

Isambard went to work with his father when he was 17. He helped to build a tunnel under the River Thames in London. In 1827, the tunnel filled with water.

The Thames Tunnel was the first tunnel to be built under a river.

Isambard worked very hard to mend the tunnel. He worked for 12 hours every day. But, the next year, the tunnel filled with water again. Isambard was badly hurt.

Isambard saved a man's life when the tunnel flooded.

The Clifton Suspension Bridge

While he was getting better, Isambard went to Bristol. He entered a competition to **design** a new bridge there. It was a very difficult job.

The bridge had to cross a deep **gorge** on the River Avon.

Isambard designed a **suspension bridge**. He won the competition. Unfortunately, there was only enough money to build part of the bridge. Isambard could not finish it.

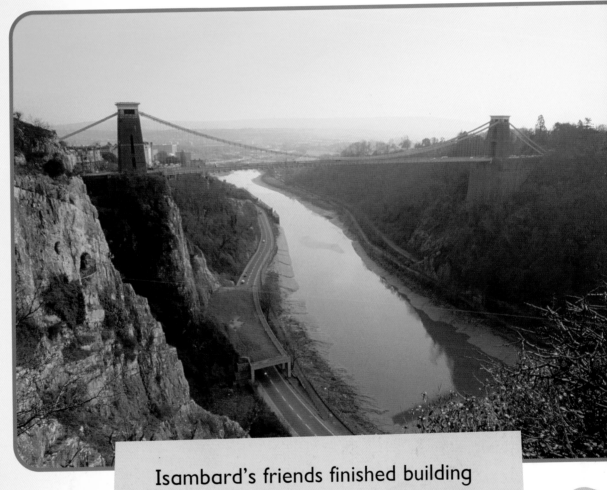

Isambard's friends finished building the bridge for him, many years later.

The Great Western Railway

When Isambard was 27, he got another important job. He was made **chief engineer** of the Great Western Railway.

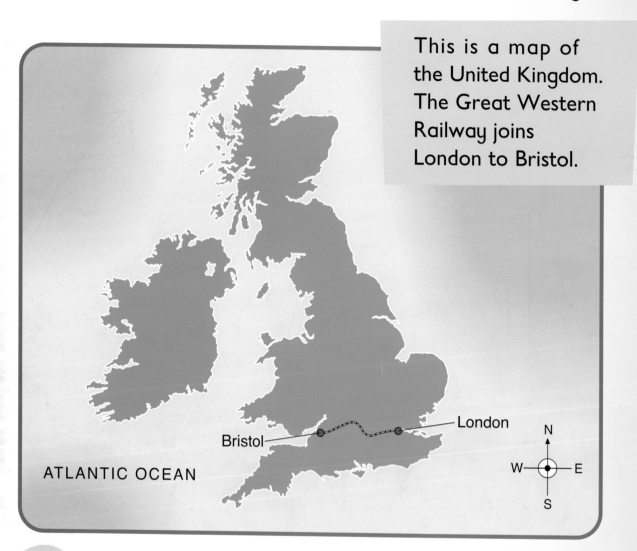

This is a map of the United Kingdom. The Great Western Railway joins London to Bristol.

London

Bristol

ATLANTIC OCEAN

N
W—E
S

Isambard **designed** a lot of things to do with the railway. He planned the tracks, the bridges, the tunnels, and even the lamp posts for the stations!

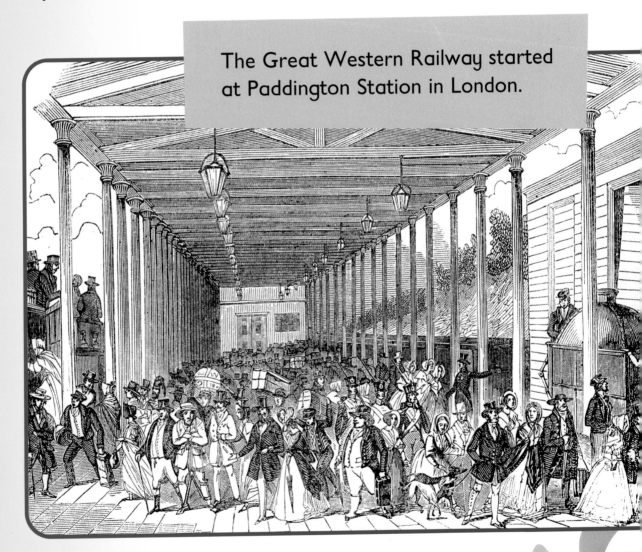

The Great Western Railway started at Paddington Station in London.

Record breakers!

The most amazing part of the Great Western Railway was the Box Tunnel. At that time, it was one of the longest tunnels in the world. It was three kilometres long.

Two teams of workmen tunnelled from each end to meet in the middle.

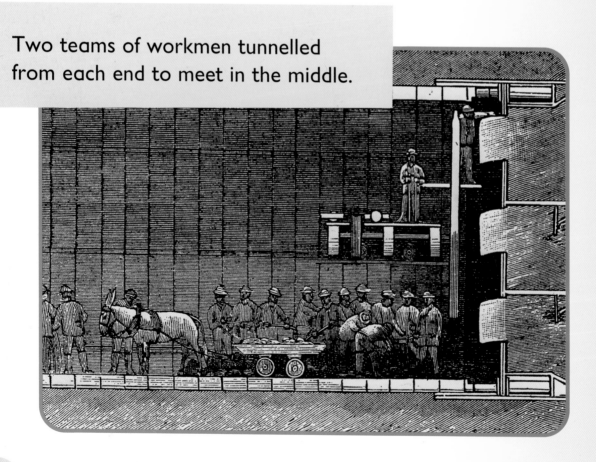

Isambard **designed** another very famous bridge, called the Maidenhead Bridge. It was also part of the Great Western Railway.

The Maidenhead Bridge had the widest and flattest brick arch in the world.

A family man

When he was 30, Isambard married Mary Horsley. They had three children. Isambard worked very hard, so he did not see much of his children.

Isambard spent most of his time working.

One day, Isambard tried to make his children laugh and swallowed a coin. It stuck in his throat, and he almost died. It took over a month to get the coin out.

Some men strapped Isambard to a board and shook the coin out.

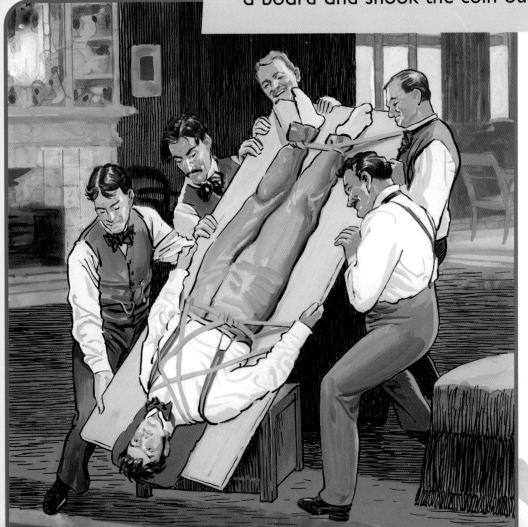

Sailing to America

Isambard wanted to build a **steamship** that could travel between England and America. People said that it could not be done. Isambard took no notice of them!

The Great Western was the first wooden steamship to sail from England to America.

People said that no ship could carry enough coal to make steam for such a long journey. In 1836 and 1837, Isambard built two big ships called *The Great Western* and *The Great Britain*.

Isambard was the first person to use **propellers** in big steamships.

War work

Isambard always wanted to make things that were new and different. In 1855, he was asked to **design** hospitals to help soldiers hurt in the **Crimean War**.

Many soldiers were being hurt in the war.

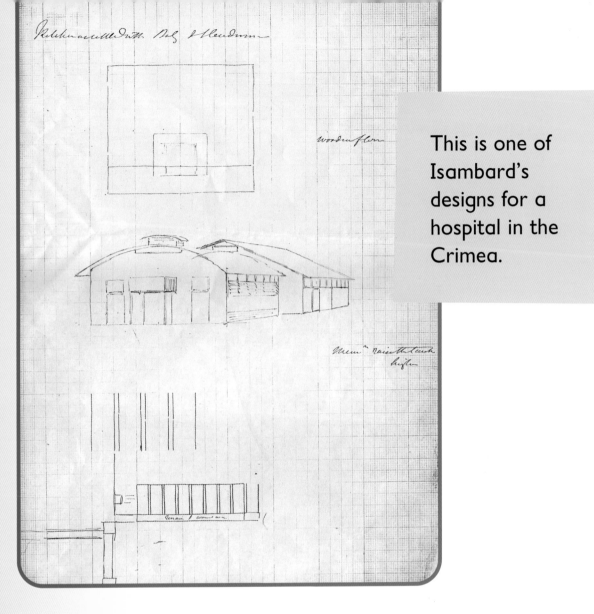

This is one of Isambard's designs for a hospital in the Crimea.

There were not enough hospitals for the soldiers. Isambard designed hospital buildings that came in pieces. The soldiers put them together near the battlefield.

The biggest ship in the world!

Isambard wanted to build the biggest ship in the world. He called it *The Great Eastern*. It would be made out of **iron**. This was a very expensive and difficult job.

Many workers were needed to build *The Great Eastern*.

The big chains behind Isambard were used to **launch** The Great Eastern.

Isambard died on 15 September 1859. He was only 53 years old. He was rich and famous, but very tired because he had worked too hard all his life.

Why is Isambard famous?

Isambard **designed** things that no one else had thought of. We still use the bridges and railway lines that he built. **Engineers** still use his ideas.

Today, trains are still made using Isambard's ideas.

In 2003, there was a television **poll** to find the Greatest Briton of All Time. Isambard Kingdom Brunel was voted number two!

There is a university, and many other places in Britain named after Isambard.

Isambard's great ship today

The *Great Britain* is now back in Bristol, in the place where it was first built. A few years ago it was falling apart.

The *Great Britain* took people to America for many years.

You can visit *The Great Britain* in Bristol.

Now the ship has been mended and painted and put in a ship **museum**. People can walk all round it and see what it looked like when it was new.

Fact file

- An **opera** has been written about Isambard's life!

- There are many places named after Isambard in Bristol. These include an Indian restaurant called the *Brunel Raj*. There are also lots of streets all over England named after Isambard. Is there one where you live?

- When *The Great Eastern* was **launched**, 3000 people came to watch. The workmen could not get the great ship into the water. One workman was killed and others were hurt.

- Isambard **designed** the Royal Albert Bridge at Saltash in Cornwall. It was opened by Queen Victoria's husband, Prince Albert, in 1859.

- The Thames Tunnel is still used today for the London Underground railway.

Timeline

1806	Isambard Kingdom Brunel is born on 9 April in Portsmouth
1826	Isambard is put in charge of work on the Thames Tunnel
1828	Isambard is badly hurt in the second tunnel flood
1829 –1831	Isambard **designs** Clifton **Suspension Bridge**
1833	Isambard is made **chief engineer** on the Great Western Railway
1836	Isambard marries Mary Horsley
1837	Isambard's first ship, *The Great Western*, is **launched**
1838	The first section of the Great Western Railway is opened *The Great Britain* is launched
1858	*The Great Eastern* is launched
1859	Isambard dies on 15 September
1864	Clifton Suspension Bridge in Bristol is opened

Glossary

chief engineer engineer in charge

Crimean War war that lasted from 1853 until 1856. Soldiers from Britain and France fought against Russian soldiers. Britain and France won the war.

design invent, usually by drawing a plan

engineer someone who designs, makes or fixes machines, bridges and so on

gorge a river valley with very steep sides

iron a type of metal

launch set off into the water (usually for the first time)

memorial something to remind us of people who have died

museum place where important pieces of art or parts of history are kept for people to see

opera a play set to music

poll when people all over the country are asked what they think about something

propeller blades that go round and round to move a ship or plane

steamship a ship moved by the power of steam. Coal was burned to boil water to make the steam.

suspension bridge a bridge that hangs from cables connected to a tower at each end

Find out more

Books

Famous People: Isambard Kingdom Brunel, 4Learning (2003)

Websites

www.bbc.co.uk/history/historic_figures

Places to visit

The Great Britain, in Bristol

Maidenhead Railway Bridge, near Maidenhead

Clifton Suspension Bridge, near Bristol

Royal Albert Bridge at Saltash, near Plymouth

Index

Titles in *The Life of* series include:

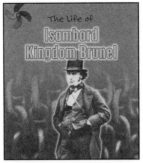

The Life of
Isambard Kingdom Brunel

Hardback   0 431 18110 1

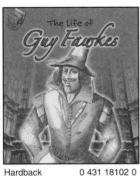

The Life of
Guy Fawkes

Hardback   0 431 18102 0

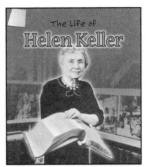

The Life of
Helen Keller

Hardback   0 431 18096 2

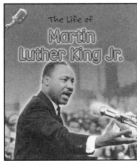

The Life of
Martin Luther King Jr.

Hardback   0 431 18095 4

The Life of
Florence Nightingale

Hardback   0 431 18093 8

The Life of
Samuel Pepys

Hardback   0 431 18104 7

The Life of
Mary Seacole

Hardback   0 431 18103 9

The Life of
Harriet Tubman

Hardback   0 431 18094 6

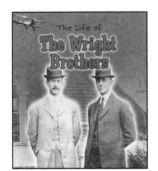

The Life of
The Wright Brothers

Hardback   0 431 18097 0

Find out about the other titles in the Heinemann Library on our website www.heinemann.co.uk/library